Life On a String

Poems and Songs
by
Stephen J. Van Hook

Glen Park Press
2016

*"Somewhere his gold sits waiting, until
And somewhere out there his spirit searches still."*

Life On A String

To Jenny, Jacob and Dietre.

Deep gratitude to my good friends and mentors Jim Colbert and Doug Irwin – two of the finest songwriters I know – for their continual encouragement and support. Thanks to Jeff Gibble, Mel DeYoung and Amalia Shaltiel for their interest in my work and constructive suggestions over the years. Additional thanks to the family and friends (too many to name individually here) who have come out to hear me perform and/or given me generous comments or helpful critiques on my poetry and music. And my heartfelt appreciation to anyone who told me that a song of mine had moved her/him – your comment made all the time spent crafting that piece worthwhile!

A special thanks to Dietre Van Hook for creating the album cover art for my last five demo CDs (one of which appears in this book), and for letting me use several drawings he made when he was younger, including the touching *Father & Son* cover for this book. And thanks to Jacob and Jenny Van Hook for the use of several of their photographs, especially adorable ones of our cat River Song.

And finally, thanks to Jim Colbert for doing the graphic design for this book and inspiring me with his own exquisite book of poetry, *Defiantly Blue Sky*.

Copyright © 2016 by Stephen J. Van Hook
All rights reserved. This book or any portion thereof may not be reproduced or used in any manner whatsoever without the express written permission of the publisher except for the use of brief quotations in a book review or scholarly journal.
First Printing: 2016
ISBN 0-9665009-2-X
Glen Park Press
690 Tanager Drive
State College, PA 16803

Introduction

On Memorial Day 2012, just home from Folk College, I decided to write a song to honor my Uncle Jim, (see pp. 65-67), who had played an important role in my life when I was a boy. That song started me down a path of songwriting (and later, poetry), for I discovered that I greatly enjoyed the process of crafting a song or poem to tell a story or convey an experience, despite frequent periods of frustration along the way. The pieces in this book (dating from May 2012 to February 2016) include reflections on my journey, responses to events in the world, true stories from history, and whimsical commentaries on everyday life. I've placed them in some rough categories:

- Flow
- Muses
- American Lives
- Newtown & Charleston & …
- True Stories
- Fatherhood
- Farewells

Nearly all of the photographs accompanying the text are my own or those taken by family and friends (see the photo credits at the end for details about each photo).

I hope you enjoy these poems/songs & photos!

Stephen J. Van Hook

Life On A String

Contents

FLOW

Yin Yang	1
Life on a String	3
On the Beach 'Round Sunrise	5
All Good Here	6
Two Strings	9
Chasing Fireflies	10

MUSES — 11

My Jesus Dorito	12
Birds, I hate you	14
A New Notebook	15
Lost Papas Fritas	16
Beauty	16
Poems	17
Still They Write On	18

AMERICAN LIVES — 20

Sunday Evening	21
Torn	21
To Do List	21
Nothing	21
Parallel Conversations, I hope	22
Maine	24
Organizing Stuff	25
Regrets	25
Jesus Drove a Cadillac	26
Sea-Faring Man	28
Target	30

NEWTOWN & CHARLESTON & …   31

Senseless   32
Us and Them   34
Symbol   35
Forgiveness   36
Jesus' Message to America   37
Root Causes   37

TRUE STORIES   38

Throws Like A Girl   39
American Hero (The Ballad of Henry Lincoln Johnson)   42
Buffalo Soldier   45
Mad King Ludwig   46
Granddad's Photo   48
Land of the Free   50

FATHERS & SONS   52

Father's Day 2015   53
The Idiot   54
Playing Catch in Ebbets Field   56
Things We Forget   58
An Autumn Hike   60
A Father's Love For His Son   62
Random Walks   64

FAREWELL   65

Uncle Jim   66
Joe Strummer   68
Raspberry Jam   69
Be A Man (Mr. Rogers)   70
Sarah Jane   72
River Song   74
The Secret   77

Photo Credits   78

Life On A String

Flow

Yin Yang

I have no dew-eyed love songs,
No "Let's get it on, Babe's."
I'm too old for all that
Now that I'm middle aged.
Just poems about little things,
Trivia that matter to me.
And songs about mature love,
Whatever that might be.

Nothing's all happy,
But nothing's all sad.
Yin Yang like life,
At least the one that I've had.
Great are the peaks, but one falls before long
& Deep truths often speak from the doldrums.
So regrets temper my happy songs
& A bit of hope shines in the dark ones.

Life on a String

Drift on the breeze, seem to float in the air,
A Tai Chi master suspended with care.
I glide like silk, hypnotically spin,
Flow not resist, I blend with the wind.

One part chases, one part flees,
Yet neither piece is taking the lead.
One may spin fast, another turn slow.
I'm always moving, but I've nowhere to go.

Red triangles & black kites
One blue anchor, or is it a wing?
All torques are balanced, each piece hanging
From its center of gravity,
My life on a string.

Pivot on pivot, countless axes,
To those below, I'm rather a tease.
Gracefully move, given my size,
One arm turns counter & another clockwise.

I'm just painted metal, yet ethereal,
Somehow I transcend my material.
A Calder creation, I weigh half a ton.
Yet I'm airy and light,
      who said art can't be fun?

Red triangles & black kites
One blue anchor, or is it a wing?
All torques are balanced, each piece hanging
From its center of gravity,
My life on a string.

Back in '76, Sandy designed me,
But he passed away, so never did see
His final creation, my life on a string,
Here in the National Gallery, East Wing.
They loved his circus, his jewelry,
La Grande Vitesse, and now of course me.

On the balcony a little blonde boy
Chases my tail, he thinks I'm a toy.
I bring joy from up here on high,
Unlike other works here,
      no one needs to ask why.

Makes me happy how others are pleased,
For just a moment, they've become
      one with me.
Drifting slowly, like a dream on the breeze,
A brief respite from all their worries.

Bet you're surprised to hear a sculpture sing
But that's my life here on a string.

On the Beach 'Round Sunrise

On the beach 'round sunrise
Go down to do Tai Chi
On the firm wet sand at low tide
As the sun creeps 'bove the sea.
The waves crash & roll up to shore
Their peaceful music bring.
At this hour nearly deserted
Just a few others doing their thing.

On the rocks some fishermen
Are hoping for a bite.
Father & little daughter
Trying to fly a kite.
Young woman in a bikini
Out for a morning swim.
Mother & preschool boy exploring
What the tide washed in.

Down the beach some yogis
Have come to salute the sun.
Then lay on the sand for *Savasana*
Once their asanas done.
A solitary surfer out to
Catch what waves she can.
Middle-aged couple out here
Strolling hand-in-hand.

On the pier a man reads his Bible
His mind on heavenly affairs,
While teenage girls go jogging by
& Wind whips 'round their hair.
Water laps an old man's toes
As they sink into the sand.
We're all just living the American dream
Here where ocean meets the land.

'Cause everyone's following their own path
Pursuing happiness for themselves
Doing what seems to work for them
And no one bothers no one else.
It's our Founder's vision realized,
America as it's meant to be:
You are free to find your own way
As you leave me to be me.

On the beach 'round sunrise
Go down to do Tai Chi
On the beach 'round sunrise
People living free.

Life On A String

All Good Here

Pass Jim Colbert sporting a bear suit.
"Hey Balladeer, can you sing me a song?"
Drives off in a Boattail Riviera,
"Been tilting at windmills all day long."

On the Green, Doug Irwin rattles the cage.
Dances with his daughter, she's still at that age.
With Grace pass 'round Chalices of Gold,
All uplifted having fed their own souls.

At the Acoustic Brew, Verlon Thompson's just played
Humming Stringbean in the chair brigade.
Erin Condo wears her Leaving Song shoes
While Monica Brindle's got the Workday Blues.

Greg Trooper hits on Mary of Scot in Queens
While she sits in Webster's eating salad greens.
Sips Le Marche tea to his thirst quench
Whispers in her ear, "Baby, I'm so French."

Yeah, it's all good here, no worries man
With Simple Gifts you'll have more fun than you can stand
Gypsy Holly, flamboyant emcee
Bob & Annie run it behind the scenes.
You may not find what you're looking for
Bet you'll find something so much more.

A ghost wanders whispering "409"
As he sees how his image has disappeared.
The old wizard pouts behind his screen
Mike the Mailman's still revered.

In the Assassin's tower, Jenny counts heads
Top of the stairs, Calder hangs by a thread.
Mouth on his harp, Richard plays the blues.
Six a.m., Mel's on air with the news.

Evan is grasping the sparrow's tail,
Flowers in her hand, Lucy guards the trail.
Amalia reels silk on the lawn as an
Angel appears, his sword drawn.

The devil strolls out of Saint's Café then
Turns into the Church across the way.
Guns drawn, cops rush to kick him out.
"All welcomed here!" Ned & Joel shout.

Yeah, it's all good here, no worries ma'am
With Callanish you'll have more fun than you can stand
Gypsy Holly, flamboyant emcee
Curtis & Johanna behind the scenes.
You may not find what you're looking for
Bet you'll find something so much more.

Yeah, you may not find what you're looking for
Bet you'll find something so much more.

Life On A String

Two Strings

Life like gravity can't keep you down
'Cause you've gotta move, you've gotta fly.
You seize the day, don't let it slip away,
Swoop & dart as you arc 'cross the sky.

You seek out those places
    where the wind gusts so fast,
Streak towards the sand, as air rushes past.
Risk of a crash in the thrill of the ride,
For in that dive you realize you're alive.

Chorus:
The more the wind blows, the higher you go.
The greater the chaos, the better your show.
'Cause living ain't something static, you know.

Your passion to create, you couldn't sate.
Fought for your life as we'd anxiously wait.
Awoke at birth covered in tubes and wires.
Now by your namesake hope you're inspired.

Little kids entranced, their parents gape
As in the air you levitate.
Life pulls and pushes, but you duck & dive,
May hit the ground hard,
    but trust you'll survive.

Chorus

Some drop from two strings to a single one
No more 'cross the sky do they dare run.
Not long 'til they're grounded
    with dim memories
Of riding the wind and the feel of the breeze.

So don't let yourself be worn down
    and eventually stop.
For striving so high, sometimes
    you're mocked.
Deflect it & fly on, don't let that voice in.
You'll regret only those runs you didn't begin.

Chorus

I'll keep the strings long,
    but keep the strings taut.
At times in the sky you're just a dot.
I'll blow as hard as I need to
So that you roam far, but never lose you.

You may fall sometimes, but that's okay.
I'll launch you back up to play.
Your spirit & the wind will do the rest.
I'll glimpse you soaring
    & know I've been blessed.

Chorus
'So off in the sky I'll watch you go.

Chasing Fireflies

Blowing bubbles & chasing fireflies
Eating fish tacos & sweet potato fries.
In front of the stage, little girls dance
By Joe Belle's singing, we're all entranced.

Eating fish tacos & sweet potato fries
On a blanket beside me, my Jenny lies.
She reads a book, while I tussle her hair
Behind us dozens are sittin' in chairs.

In front of the stage, little girls dance.
At the Lemont Village Green, none look askance.
Jenny sips Yuengling, I'm drinking Stout.
Look up to see stars peeking out.

By Joe Belle's singing, we're all entranced.
Spirit in the air echoes Van Zandt's.
Music floats over us, though it's got wings,
As Joe's fingers pluck guitar strings.

Blowing bubbles & chasing fireflies
Kids run 'round as the sunlight dies.
His last song over, Joe flashes a grin,
Then thanks the crowd & the sound men.

Next week Jim Colbert & Doug Irwin
So come next Friday, we'll be back here again.
Eating fish tacos & sweet potato fries
Blowing bubbles & chasing fireflies
Blowing bubbles & chasing fireflies.

Muses

My Jesus Dorito

My wife went to church this gorgeous Sunday morning
not appreciating that I chose to appreciate
God's creation from the back deck.

I'm mindlessly eating Doritos,
when a chip catches my eye.
In the pattern of the nacho cheese stuff
I see the face … of Jesus.
And wonder, "What the heck?"

I do marvel at this blessing,
this miraculous sign from God.
Though, as I'm skipping worship, I feel like I'm a fraud.

Still I know that devout pilgrims
will come from miles away
cheerfully give me offerings.
Before I auction it someday.

Then I consider that God may have given this gift
for me to preach some message to the world -
but is it to condemn or to uplift?

I await some guidance.
But the Dorito is silent.

Now I panic for I have nothing of substance to say.
My wife will attest to this.
My kids, too, I'm afraid.

And the Dorito is still frustratingly silent,
no matter how hard I stare,
awaiting enlightenment.

And thus my wife returns from worship
 quite surprised to find
 her husband – mesmerized -
 by a nacho chip.

"It's my Jesus Dorito," I simply explain.
"It's a sign whose meaning I must ascertain."

Just the slightest lift of an eyebrow
 indicates she is deciding
 what of this to tackle first,
 or to pretend she'd never heard.
 I see the image of a padded room
 begin forming in her mind.
"A sign of what?" is how she finally replies.

And before I can think of an answer
 - a *profound* answer, mind you -
 the chip she signals me to hand her
 so this miracle she can view.

"How do you know it's Jesus?"
 after one look she inquires.
"No one knows what he looked like,
 Something your claim would seem to require."
 Then she squints her eyes in order
 to study it even closer.
"You know," she adds, grinning,
"It looks like Elvis more."

Of course, it doesn't look like Elvis.
 It's obviously Jesus.
 She's just being ridiculous,
 so I ask. "How was church?"

"Oh, a gorgeous choral anthem.
 And at the front some fine bouquets.
 Though bit too long a sermon
 for a full communion Sunday.
 A pity that you missed it
 – 'cause with your behavior lately,
 you need all the sacramental
 help that you can get!"

With that, she walks into the kitchen,
 leaving me alone with this gift God given
 still struggling to understand
 the meaning of this vision
 on this chip now in my hand.

So I take my Jesus Dorito,
 & eat my piece of Christ.
 Then wash it down
 with Mountain Dew,
 the closest to wine at hand.
 Perhaps it did suffice.

Now, God, if you do have a message,
 I'm willing to help you spread it.
 Only please just write it down.

Oh, and if you like Doritos,
 feel free to come on 'round.

Birds, I hate you

Birds
I hate you.
Outside my window dim.
Your symphony I'd appreciate,
But it's only 5 am.

So I can only assume
That you've come here to taunt.
Know that I was up past 2
Struggling to write a song.
Oh, how its melody eluded me,
And its meter just all wrong.
Each lyric too tired a cliché
To capture what I'd want.

So at this ungodly hour
You've come to waken me
Just to flaunt how easy
To write a song can be.

Well!
Two can play at that!
Oh diminished dinosaurs.
You'll regret you ever fucked with me.
I'm sending out the cat.

A New Notebook

The joy of a new notebook,
Saying farewell to an old friend.
Record of months' worth of thoughts
Some fine, some, well, less so.
Still that's me on those pages
Projected in black & white
Scratched out & edited
Rough drafts, as I truly am,
Few polished as I wish to be.

Which of the blank books
In my closet
Shall I choose?
Which is worthy of my thoughts?
& Which is too good for them right now?
Saving those for that day
When I grow
Deep Thoughts
Worthy for display.

The blank book inviting
Infinite possibilities
Of songs to be written there.
And thus so terrifying
What first to put down?
Its opening mark –
Blemish or blessing? –
So I hesitate, unsure,
Paralyzed momentarily.
Yes, the hardest part of writing
Can be choosing the first word.

Lost Papas Fritas

If I was sure of one thing
It was where you were, poem.
First read you over 20 years ago,
One of the finest that I'd known.
I wanted to show you to my mother
To share the joy of you tonight
So I took your volume off the shelf
"Old friend," I thought,
"You welcome sight."

I looked in the index and then I looked again
Disturbed to find you nowhere listed.
Thought that maybe your title I'd forgotten.
Certainly, no doubt that you existed.
Though I confess I don't remember you
     in detail
Just that you were refreshingly short
And spoke of papas fritas.
Their curative powers, of course.

I leafed through the book quickly
Then not so fast
     Then - painstakingly - slow.
But you are not there
     & you must be I know.
I clearly recall reading you in this very book.
Bought in Socorro, New Mexico, at 22.
So what am I to make of my other memories?
Ones less sure than I was of you?

Beauty

Beauty.
I don't need to own you,
Hold, touch or photograph you.
I am just pleased
That my life you graced
For a brief, fleeting moment
& Hope you'll bless me
Once again before long,
Whether in a painting, sunset,
Person, smile or song.

Poems

Poems capture instants
  That once did occur,
      Several blended together
         & Some never were.

Ones I visited
    in fantasies
        in nightmares
           in dreams.

A recipe of illusions
      Blurred with realities.
A murky brew
      Of dubious ingredients
         Memories dimly seen,
    In ill-defined portions,
Chopped up, tossed 'round,
      Sifted, twisted,
         Sanded, pared down.

A dollop of my childhood,
 A slice of last year,
     A pinch of an old girlfriend
      Dash of unspoken fears.
Sprinkled with disappointments,
     Rejections & loss,
Soured by frustrations,
     Of gold perceived dross.

Sweetened by young children;
    Sooner than you know,
        Pride & sadness mixed in
     From watching them grow.
Spiced with ecstasy of passion
      Times we did fly.
  Yet bitter from life's limits
     To console, satisfy.

So is that poem about you?
     Well yes & no.
You're in there somewhere
     But what part?
        Even I may not know.
  What lines fit you best
     Vary by mood & whether
    Or not
It's been a good day,
    So don't read it as though
       To you some message
          I planned to convey.

What I'm saying is this:
    Whatever makes you happy,
     I wrote about you.
    And everything else
      Was written,
        You see,
     'bout somebody else.

Still They Write On

Under the covers, with a flashlight
Molly at 16 writes poems every night.
Keeps them secret
Nobody knows
That stories pour out of her
In meter & prose.
Once shared her work with a teacher she liked
His "Juvenile" silenced her voice.
20 years later, boxes she's filled.
For one who will cherish them
She's waiting still.

"Why do you write?" her voice of doubt cuts.
"No one reads them, your poems are no good."
But those stories inside her, cry out to be born
If she didn't release them, then apart she'd be torn.
She may have no talent, it may be long gone
But those stories cry out,
So still she writes on.

Duncan wakes early, stays up late at night
Driven to the keyboard, a novel to write.
10 manuscripts
Countless rejections
His girl doesn't get
Why all this he's done.
'Cause Jess can't feel how those stories possess him,
Most days he doesn't even understand it himself.
Not good enough to realize his dreams,
Yet still he pursues them
& Somedays he screams.

'Cause those stories are deeper than he can convey
Meant for a real writer, but went astray.
Should let them pass on, but they want to play.
And it's not his fault
That they passed his way.

Lexie at 40, stands at the mike
Dreams that her songs will connect tonight.
But there's blank stares on faces,
To their own talking glued
She yearns to find
One person moved.
Knows she's no Townes, no Guy or Lucinda,
No Nanci, Iris, Cohen or Dylan.
So how dare she have the audacity to try?
But out to her
Those stories still cry.

"Why do you write?" her voice of doubt cuts.
"No one listens, your songs are no good."
But those stories inside her, cry out to be born
If she didn't release them, then apart she'd be torn.
She may have no talent, it may be long gone
But those stories cry out,
So still she writes on.

Those stories cry out,
Still they write on.
'Cause those stories cry out,
So still they write on.
And on, and on, and on and on …

American Lives

Sunday Evening

Mr. Kristofferson, I beg to differ
About Sunday mornings.
For it's not then one feels the truest despair,
But, rather, Sunday evenings
When the hope of the open weekend
Has crashed into the hard reality
Of the infinite undone.

Sunday morning still bears promise
That which weighs down, long overdue,
Can, with heroic effort, finally be removed.
But Sunday evening:
The impossibly optimistic list
Has so little checked off
– Especially those starred and
Underlined as vital –
& Too late to gird one's loins
To tackle any now,
Especially given how
One's energy has decayed,
Ebbed away for the day.

Only thing left to do
Is sink deep into one's chair
While listening to the Folk Show,
Jim Colbert's voice from the radio
Coming through the air.

Torn

Torn between two important tasks,
I ended up doing neither.
Rather I dithered & frittered away
My day on assorted trifles;
For doing either one
Meant neglecting the other,
And since both were
Equally urgent,
I ignored them both
In equal measure.

To Do List

My to do list for
Today: To finally get
My shit together.

Nothing

Nothing.

Nothing happened today.

Of course, somewhere
To someone
Something happened.

But not here
& not to me.

Parallel Conversations, I hope

I hope that we were having parallel conversations
In the bar tonight.
As Jon Vickers-Jones was introducing
A story, by a slave girl, in her own words.
He said we (& we all were white)
Can't really understand
What it's like to be African-American
& then your disparaging remark we heard.

Perhaps it wasn't addressed to Jon at all,
But to a fellow poker player.
Perhaps you weren't paying even slight attention
To the open mike.
Just like we were ignoring
Your poker game this night.

The apparent link between Jon's prologue
And your comment
A mere coincidence,
I hope.
An illusion of intersection
Of two parallel
Conversations.

Unphased, Jon continued,
"We don't know what it's like to be a slave."
& Just then you said, "boo hoo"
In that same loud mocking voice.
Whether we were parallel
Or intersecting,
I couldn't help
But wonder, once again.

A confrontation would have caused a scene
& just led to more abuse -
Verbal, certainly,
Physical likely, too.
And what if that "boo hoo" had really been addressed
To a gambler at your table?
To someone who'd bet big,
Whose bluff you'd finally called.
& In his wound of ego and coin
You were tossing salt.

Whether parallel or intersecting,
I hope you listened to Jon's story
For he told it oh so well.
And you'd have learned something,
About humanity for a spell.

Maine

Buying that TV our biggest mistake
Followed by cable with endless channels
Then that pair of large, comfy recliners
Laptops & wifi, Netflix on demand.

That island in Maine is our only hope
Where you stayed one summer, as a teenager.
That one your uncle lived on, with no electricity
No wifi, TV & such luxuries.

Let's move there now, dear, before it's too late
We'll hike & read books, do puzzles, play games.
Make music, make love, reconnect with each other
Hear again our inner voices & put pen to paper.

Organizing Stuff

Organizing stuff
I never should have bought
Wish I didn't have
Will never use again.

So too busy to read a good book
Or sing a love song.
To wander in the woods
Or play with you, son.

Regrets

There's much I regret buying
Sitting in my house.
But very little I didn't buy
That I regret now.
If only I could remember this
When I see the next shiny thing
& Stay my hand before back home
Another regret I bring.

Jesus Drove a Cadillac

Jesus drove a Cadillac
Loved to watch it glide.
Interior pitch black
White on the outside.
Ramblin' all around the town
Always with the top down.
His arm around Mary Mag
Cruising down the drag.
Sure deserved a classy ride
Did the Savior of humankind
After dying for our sins
He just needed to unwind.

Jesus drove a Cadillac,
The slickest you could find.
As he was the Son of God,
No one seemed to mind.

Still recall that day he came
In glory from on high
In his Caddy he descended
Down here from the sky.
We all feared it was a sign
That the world would end,
But he said, "This ain't no apocalypse.
"I'm just hanging out, my friend."
We figured he'd be preachy
Guilt us for our sins,
But he was such a righteous dude
Had such a peaceful grin.

Jesus drove a Cadillac,
The slickest you could find.
As he was the Son of God,
No one seemed to mind.

"Folks, be cool & get along,"
He'd say when someone asked.
But mostly he just drove around
In his Cadillac.
Honored guest at every wedding
Turning water into wine,
Wherever he & Mary went
Couldn't help but be divine.
But if you were troubled or upset
With them you could confide
And always happy to oblige
If you thumbed a ride.

Jesus drove a Cadillac,
The slickest you could find.
As he was the Son of God,
No one seemed to mind.

Televangelists came to him
But Mary told them off.
"You make us miss those Pharisees,
And all they did was scoff."
Preacher tried to scold him once
Said, "You're leading them astray.
We need you to play the part
We've scripted for this day."
But Jesus said, "I did that once &
They nailed me on a cross.
Then my words by you were twisted,
My grace & love you tossed."

One day we saw him & Francis
Swapping tales about his Dad.
All night long such merriment,
What a party they all had.
& The very last we saw of them
As farewell they all waved
Jesus, Francis, Mary Mag
Sporting pince-nez shades.
Though they left, we're doing fine
For he's still in our lives,
We realized where there's love & laugher
Surely Christ abides.

Jesus drove a Cadillac,
The slickest you could find.
As he was the Son of God,
No one seemed to mind.

Now somewhere out there on the road
That Holy trio rides
& If you pass them say hello
For they say that God
    Pro-o-o-o-
        O-o-o-o-
            Vides.

Life On A String

Sea-Faring Man

Jacob was a sea-faring man, but he lived in Iowa,
The land of corn & rolling hills, the ocean he never saw.
To the dairy at 5 am, he'd drive his white truck,
Stop at every house in town, their empties he'd pick up.
And leave behind the freshest milk one could ever taste,
The kind you want to savor & never drink in haste.
Jacob was always singing as he drove around:
Old sea shanties, pirate ballads, of treasure to be found.

Jacob grew up 'round there, never outside the Midwest,
Yet sailed on the Seven Seas, each night he took his rest.
A swashbuckler was Jacob, as he rode the roaring foam,
A valiant explorer of waters unknown.
His love was a mermaid, whom he'd visit in his dreams,
Met that day he walked the plank for foiling Black Beard's schemes.
She'd guide his ship to places no human'd ever seen,
And in the surf they'd frolic like two kids in their teens.

Then dawn approached in Iowa, too soon he must wake.
& Each time he left, her heart it did break.

Jacob, oh Jacob, please stay here with me.
Don't go away again dear, one night she did plea.
Jacob, oh Jacob, please stay here with me.
Tears streaming down her face, as she begged him not to leave.
Then one morning the milk bottles stayed empty
& Jacob's body was found in bed by the sheriff's deputy.
He left behind no next of kin, and they all thought it sad,
For in his house they found a shrine to the life he wish he'd had.

An elaborate model of a schooner, in paintings it sailed free,
Journals of his voyages on this ship, the Zuider Zee.
His will was quite simple, only two items if you please:
A porthole window in his coffin & be buried at sea.
Now Jacob rides the ocean currents for eternity,
And together with his mermaid lover he can finally be.
He's looking out that porthole window, at her eyes so green,
'Cause Jacob was a sea-faring man, at least in his dreams.
Yeah, Jacob was a sea-faring man, … at least in … his dreams.

Life On A String

Target

Coming home Friday evening
In the car alone
Find myself driving past Target
Know in not to go.
For my head says,
"Surely, you need nothing,
You have too much already.
And after your long day,
I know you're rather spent."
But the pull of something
- That emptiness seeking filling -
Was just too strong a feeling
And so in I went.

There had been a pair of shorts I liked
But sadly not in my size
Last time I was in the store
Just two days before.
So I went to that rack first
To justify my coming
Alas, my size still absent
And still I needed filling,
Thus I found myself
On an indirect
Route back to the door.

I drifted through the sporting goods
The toys, the Legos,
Kitchen gadgets,
& Gardening tools.
Deck furniture, beach gear,
Pool toys that promised leisure.
Storage bins that promised structure.

I looked at every BluRay
And scanned every DVD
Hoping to find a movie
That I would want to see.
Something that could briefly
Plug the hole
I felt so keenly.

But nothing sang its Siren song
Except at the checkout.
An overpriced Diet Coke,
Of Diet Dew they were out.
Though I knew I wouldn't enjoy it
That in the end 'twould go to waste.
Again my head unheeded
For this drink I felt I needed.
The cold & the bite of carbonation
My mouth irresistibly craved,
But after a few sips,
Was no longer to my taste.

That half hour gone forever
That time spent wandering wasted,
As if somehow something in that store
Could have joy in me created.
Why had I not continued on home
To read a good book, cat in lap?
And not fallen yet once again
For this possessions trap?

Newtown & Charleston & ...

Senseless

We'd decorated the tree the night before
Now its lights stay dark, needles collect on the floor.
My angel costume still hangs in the hall
Near Bobby Jr.'s photo on the wall.
My twin brother was to be a shepherd
In our pageant, but our lives were shattered.
Now baby Jesus and Santa are no more
And the Hanukkah lights have gone out next door.

Chorus: (after every verse):
Hold tight my kitty, feel his heart beat
As I lay here hiding under the sheet.
That monster comes for me every night
In my dreams, I cry out in fright.
Kitty's the only one I can tell what's in my head
I don't understand why my brother's dead.

Miss Davis pleads for our lives
Tries to protect us, "Just children!" she cries.
A blast in my ears & she collapses on the floor
Then he turns on us, all twenty-four.
Bobby grabs me, we desperately flee,
Hide in a corner, Bobby covers me.
I can hear each shot and just pray in vain
Bobby cries out, and I feel a sharp pain.

Mom called Bobby a handful
Dad said he'd be a defensive tackle.
Always playing tricks, he sure could be wild,
I'm sorry I wished I were an only child.

Bobby played sick, but mom knew better,
Then dad yelled at him, called him a liar.
Now they argue about who's to blame
That they made him go, didn't play his game.

Mom's broken up, she can't stop crying,
In her mind, she keeps seeing him dying.
Attacked the gun cabinet with a chair
Threw out our toy ones in despair.
I asked mom why such things exist
Why he'd want to hurt us, why couldn't he have missed?
I asked why God allowed this to happen
She turned away, afraid of my question.

Dad ignores me, just sits and drinks,
How it could have been different I know he thinks.
He keeps muttering that if only he'd been there
Could have saved Bobby Jr., & stopped this nightmare.
Now he just sits and fingers his gun
Imagining he was there saving everyone.
Late one night saw him point-it near his eye
When he put it down, finally heard him cry.

I want Bobbie back, no monster in dreams,
Mom to smile & laugh again,
Dad to stop drinking & feeling mad
At himself, at our world so sad.
I wish that monster had left us alone
Never had to see Bobby Jr.'s headstone.
We never teased him or called him names
So why did he do it, why did us he blame?

I don't understand why my brother's dead.

Life On A String

Us and Them

Black & White
A biological fiction
A social construction
Over which we kill each other.
Hating our cousins
For things superficial
Like a distant parent's birthplace
Or what we choose to wear
With whom we fall in love
Or what name we call our God.

Over this we choose
To tear apart lives
& Lay our hatred bare.
And so we mourn once again
In that grief-filled ritual
Where nothing can be said
& We cannot understand why.

We were *just* here
For the last one,
For children cut down,
Young lives truncated
Their mothers' cries still echo
& Harmonize
With cries begun anew.

And we pray sober in the knowledge
We'll be back here again soon
Until we all erase
The "them"
From our minds
For "they" are just "us",
All God's children,
One humankind.

Symbol

Its red triangles stained
By the blood of its victims,
Killed for its vision
Of hatred and division.
The white hood
And burning cross
Vile terror,
Tragic life loss.
All in Christ's name,
Taken
So in vain.

That strange fruit hanging,
Dripping, from a tree
Down in Texas, Alabama,
Mississippi.
Red Summer to keep us
Up on our perch.
Four sweet girls bombed
In a Birmingham church.
Out of Medgar Evers,
His life we did wring.
We beat those in Selma,
Martyred God's prophet
Dr. King.

Now there's fresh new blood
From nine Godly souls
Spilled by a young man
Who too well understood
What this flag meant &
For what it stood.

Yet we still wave it
Wear it on our shirts
On our pickup trucks
Knowing whom it hurts.
We're just some good old boys
Never meaning no harm
As if the blood encrusted
Were just Southern charm.
Like the noose, the shackle,
Slave auction, slave ship.
We say we're all past that now,
As we wield
The bull whip.

Forgiveness

I know it's not right that I hold tight my anger
While those who suffered unspeakable grief
Can somehow, in Christ's name, offer forgiveness,
And witness to us a perplexingly deep faith,
Of belief unshaken at quake epicenter
As they faced
Their loved ones' killer
And offered God's love.
While I, a mere distant observer,
Still cling to my hate,
Something those in Nickel Mines, Pennsylvania,
And now Charleston, South Carolina,
Filled with God's spirit
Have risen above.

Jesus' Message to America
(Recent events have caused Him to break His long silence)

America,
Don't confuse your faith in me
For love of your guns,
Or ignore my call to help the needy
'Cause they differ from you, dear ones.
"Love your neighbor as yourself"
Extends beyond your next door.
Recall I was hungry and homeless –
And how my plight you did ignore?

Is your security in our Heavenly Father
Or in the borders you secure?
Your trust in the Rock of Ages,
Or in the walls you build in fear?
As you tread through valleys of shadow,
Where veiled whispers hint at harm,
Where do you lean for comfort:
On me, or on your arms?

Facing a future hidden from view,
Succumb not to the voice of Hate,
Who feeds the darkness inside you;
Rather, trust in my Amazing Grace.
Brothers & sisters, strive to be
Whom your ideals speak about.
How can others learn to follow
If your hope gives way to doubt?

I planted you a beacon,
A light to this storm-tossed Earth,
A signal flare in its despair
To unite, not break apart.
In love I say, come follow me,
Not those who sow fear.
So, pray for peace, my dears,
And then
Open
Your hearts.

Root Causes

Some say mental health,
Others racism & guns.
But while we argue over root causes
We're doing diddly-squat
About each one.
High schoolers at Columbine
Cried out for us to get the job done.
As did the children of Newtown
& Church goers in Charleston.
Theater patrons in Aurora
& College kids in Oregon.
"Please, let us be the last!"
To us they've all pled.
But our hands we've wrung
& Our requisite tears
We've already shed.
Lip service paid to root causes
Mental health, racism, or guns.
And again, no lessons drawn
And quickly we move on.

True Stories

Throws Like a Girl

Second of April, 1931,
Delayed by rain, but today there was sun.
Chattanooga Lookouts, class AA,
Faced the mighty Yankees, an exhibition game.

Lookouts pitcher Barfoot first inning didn't last
Whom they brought out, caused many to laugh.
Who would face Babe Ruth, that home-run machine?
Why a wiry little southpaw, just a girl of 17.

Jackie Mitchell stood there powdering her nose.
Her excitement, her fear, she dared not expose.
Had a wicked drop pitch, it'd plunge like a rock.
Raised in baseball since she could walk.
Scattering of catcalls as they tossed her the ball.

Jackie, oh Jackie, bet you throw like a girl
This ain't no game for makeup and pearls.
Don't you know that girls are too frail?
To play pro ball, you're destined to fail.
They laugh 'cause you try to play with the men.

The Babe stood at the plate, grin on his face.
Ready to put this girl in her place.
He tipped his hat, and she wound-up tight
Ruth watched for a ball, didn't like the height.

Next pitch he swung, but the ball was not there.
"Strike 1" the Ump called, Babe gave him a glare.
On her third pitch, he swung hard & fast
"Strike 2" the Ump boomed as the ball swished past.

Life On A String

With a look of cold steel, Ruth was poised to spring,
But the next pitch passed without his swing.
"Strike 3, you're out!" the Ump declared.
Like a sudden inferno, Babe's anger flared.
Flung down in disgust, his bat as he cussed.

Jackie, oh Jackie, you throw like a girl
Guess that means that you can sure hurl.
Didn't you know that girls are too frail?
They all said you were destined to fail.
But you put them in their place & you did it with grace.

The crowd roared for Jackie, how she did astound,
Except for some men, who grimaced and frowned.
Surely a bad call or a practical joke.
No girl could ever strike out such a bloke.

For satisfaction they wouldn't have to wait, 'cause
Iron Horse Lou Gehrig was next at the plate.
Despite just seeing the homerun king fall,
No doubt that Gehrig would slaughter that ball.

In the batter's box, Gehrig dug in his treads.
Ball in her hand, Jackie fingered the threads.
Next pitch her focus, pushed her nerves aside,
Crowd all felt pressure building inside.
It was over in three pitches: three swings, three misses.

Jackie, oh Jackie, you throw like a girl
Guess that means that you can sure hurl.
Didn't you know that girls are too frail?
They all said you were destined to fail.
Now the women grin, 'cause you struck out the men.

All rose at once to cheer Jackie that day, but
In the newspaper, Babe was quoted to say:
"Women are too delicate. It would kill them to play,
Just too frail to play ball every day."
Men whispered that it was an April Fool's prank:
"Couldn't really happen, let us be frank."
Claimed Babe and Gehrig must have taken a fall
For a publicity stunt, that's all.

Then two days later, the baseball commish
Voided her contract, said girls were unfit.
Why women were fragile, not up to the strain,
And it was unseemly, debased the game.
Won't tolerate this spectacle, he did proclaim.

Jackie, oh Jackie, you throw like a girl
Guess that means that you can sure hurl.
Are you touched by men's concern for you?
That they banned you from doing what you love to do?
Yeah, they've kicked out the women 'cause you struck out the men.

But every so often, she'd haunt the Babe's dreams.
"Sure galls you to fall to a real Babe in her teens.
Saw that steel in your eye, how you'd wanted that ball.
Don't you dare deny you were aiming for the wall.
Think we're so fragile 'cause we ain't got your girth?
Let's see how you'd handle childbirth.
Yeah, Let's see how you'd handle childbirth."

Oh, Jackie, oh Jackie, 'fraid this is the end.
They've kicked out the women 'cause you struck out the men.
Yeah, they've kicked out the women, 'cause you struck out the men.

American Hero
(The Ballad of Henry Lincoln Johnson)

Fifth Avenue, on a cold winter morn
Hundreds march triumphantly in uniform.
In tight formation, helmets glisten
To Big Jim's jazz band everyone listens.
A million strong along the parade route
Wives and mothers to their men shout.
Those Harlem Hellfighters have finally come home
From the Great War, such bravery shone.
And beaming in a car, with a bouquet of flowers
Is Henry Johnson the man of the hour.

Chorus:
'Cause Henry Johnson's an American hero
Fought off two dozen Germans one night
Twenty-one wounds yet kept up the fight.
One of the five bravest men of the war
So said our President T.R.
Henry Johnson: American Hero!
Henry Johnson: American Hero!

They couldn't march to war with the Rainbow division.
"No black in a rainbow" the reason given.
Loaded coal, laid railroad tracks,
'Cause Pershing refused combat to blacks.
They insisted on fighting, so he gave 'em to the French.
As the 369th they manned that trench.
That May evening, at Post 29
Henry & Needham Roberts were guarding the line.
France was sure far from Albany
Where Henry'd been a porter for the railroad.
Tonight he sensed trouble, danger forbode.

That moonlit night, heard a wire cutter's snip
Henry fired all three bullets in his clip.
A barrage of grenades, how the shrapnel did burn.
Wounded, Needham threw grenades in return.
Germans came at them from both sides.
One fired a Lugar, hit Henry in the thigh.
No time to reload, had to act or be dead.
Swinging his rifle, cracked that German on the head.

Saw another carrying Needham away
With his Bolo knife, that Bush he slayed.
German with the Lugar started shooting him again.
Drove that bolo knife through his stomach, gutting him.
The Bushes fled back over no man's land
Henry threw hand grenades as they ran.
"Corporal of the Guard!" he yelled, collapsing on the floor.
"I'm okay," said later. "I've been shot before."

Chorus

Pride for the Hellfighters everyone did share,
France awarded them its Croix de Guerre.
"They never retreat. Go forward or die,"
Colonel Hayward said, then they reached the Rhine.
Once they took ground, never let it go.
To the Kaiser gave a crushing blow.
191 days of combat in the war,
No other Americans served any more.
And the best damn regiment ragtime band
With James Reese Europe sowing jazz in France.

Henry died a broken man in '29
Divorced & drunk, what a sad decline.
Been unable to work 'cause of war injuries
Buried in Arlington Cemetery.

Life On A String

Honored in France with their highest award
But valor of black men our army ignored.
Eighty years later, finally made a start
Distinguished Service Cross & Purple Heart.
But the Medal of Honor they still deny.
One wonders why.
One wonders why.

'Cause Henry Johnson's an American hero
Fought off two dozen Germans one night
Twenty-one wounds yet kept up the fight.
One of the five bravest men of the war
So said our President T.R.
Henry Johnson: American Hero!
Henry Johnson: American Hero!

Author's note: I wrote this song in June 2013 when I came across his story researching a song about African-American soldiers in WW I (which became *Land of the Free*). Two years later, on June 2nd, 2015, President Barack Obama posthumously awarded Henry Lincoln Johnson the Medal of Honor.

Note on terminology: The Harlem Hellfighters called the German soldiers "Bush" (or "Bushes"), a variation on Bosch, a term the French soldiers used for the Germans.

Buffalo Soldier

Buffalo soldier, why do you fight?
You too've felt oppression's bite.
By treaty all this land is Sioux,
Now there's gold, they want it, too.

Red Cloud refused Grant's demand
To abandon our birth land.
With Sitting Bull & Crazy Horse
We resist with all our force.

We fight for more than our lives,
To ensure our world survives.

Buffalo Soldier, you've traveled far
Just to take this land of ours.
Savages they call us Sioux.
What names do they use for you?

They dragged you in chains to this soil
In cotton fields they made you toil.
Sold your child, defiled your wife.
Why help 'em steal our way of life?

We have a common enemy.
Buffalo soldier, can't you see?

Buffalo soldier, buffalo soldier,
You are brave and so are we.
Buffalo soldier, buffalo soldier,
We both fight for liberty.
Buffalo soldier, buffalo soldier,
We ask only to be free.

Buffalo soldier, they wish us dead
But they hate black as much as red.
All the proof that you need
Is swinging from a Texas tree.

Millions just fought to keep you down
Just because your skin is brown.
Their whip scars still show on your back
Think you're nothing 'cause your skin is black.

You and we are more alike
Than those whose skin is white.

Buffalo soldier, buffalo soldier,
You are brave and so are we.
Buffalo soldier, buffalo soldier,
We both fight for liberty.
Buffalo soldier, buffalo soldier,
We ask only to be free.

We live only when we're free.

Mad King Ludwig

The 19th century's not for me, I hearken to the past.
The middle ages as it was, or how it should have been.
Medieval Romantic revelries, brave & chivalrous knights.
A world apart from all that's coarse in Munich and Berlin.
If I can't live in that reality, I'll create the fantasy.
My brother's in the asylum, yet mad they call me.
I'm Mad King Ludwig, Lord of Bavaria!

My father Maximillian was a real king, they say,
But I'm the one they still remember fondly to this day.
Whose castle do they come from around the world to see?
There's nothing more impressive from Austria to the Spree.
They mocked my romantic visions, but who's laughing now?
My face is on the postcards, on the steins my noble brow.
I'm Mad King Ludwig, Lord of Bavaria!

I'm Parsifal, the Grail King, in my throne room they all drool.
God on the ceiling blesses my sacred rule.
You've surely seen my Neuschwanstein, if only a photo.
Come check out my Linderhof, you'll love the grotto.
Where in my boat they row me 'round, for I'm the swan king.
Listen to Wagner's operas, hear Tannhäuser sing.
My chandelier's more Meissen than you've ever seen.
I'm the Sun King reincarnated, another Louis XIV.
I'm Mad King Ludwig, Lord of Bavaria!

Take after my *Grossvater*, who started Oktoberfest.
'Til they made him abdicate his crown for the one whom he loved best.
I'm the moon king, for I always reign at night.
The love I feel dare not reveal itself in the daylight.
Like Tristan und Isolde, my passion's deep and strong
Their tragic love on my bedroom walls inspires me to song.
I'm Mad King Ludwig, Lord of Bavaria!

The path of the Kaiser led to a World War
While my own road of fantasy led to tourists galore.
Say I'm a Fairy tale king living in a dream.
But all I really wanted was some Bavarian crème.
I'm Mad King Ludwig, Lord of Bavaria!
Yes, I'm Mad King Ludwig, Lord of Bavaria!

Granddad's Photo

A framed photo hung over granddad's dresser
Of a simple lunch counter, from an old newspaper.
Just sitting there, young women & men,
While a crowd for some reason was shouting at them.
On my ninth birthday I asked him, why those standing were so mad.
"'Cause people seen as different dared sit," said granddad.

"See that counter was whites-only & some sitting were black,
When I was your age, were many places like that.
'Course black folks objected, and even some whites,
And by sitting down, stood up for what was right.
But many feared change, wanted things as they were,
Hit and spit at those seated, while yelling slurs."

"Why, seems so silly," I had to say.
"Because of skin color treat someone that way."
"Pleased to hear you say that," granddad replied.
"Gives me hope that past evils may someday die.
I see in you how we've come far since then.
Though clearly not there, proved time and again."

I asked "Are you in this photo?" and he nodded yes.
Which of the two white men seated I tried to guess.
"You're looking in the wrong place," he finally said.
To one of those shouting, he pointed instead.
I looked up at him, sure he was playing a joke.
"That's me, at eighteen," he quietly spoke.

"On that day," he said, "I framed this with pride.
But as time past, I slowly realized
How wrong I had been and so hid it in shame.
Found it years later, and hung it up with the aim:
To be a constant reminder to never again
Let my perception fail to penetrate beyond other's skin."

"How I had let myself succumb to hate instead
Of loving my neighbor as the Lord Himself said.
To always forgive others, recalling my own past sin,
To now stand for justice, which always will win."
As if a delicate flower, the photo, he handed to me.
Said, "the Future's in your hands, make it good, make it free.
It's up to you to determine what kind of world this'll be.
I'm giving this to you, girl, to be wiser than me.
Yeah, I'm counting on you to be wiser than me."

Life On A String

Land of the Free

Born in Georgia, fled soon as I could
Up to Detroit where the work was good.
And no more cowards under white hoods.
      When the call came to fight the Hun
      For democracy, for freedom.
      I answered though liberty
      Had been so often denied me. *Had been denied me.*

Proud to live in the land of the free,
I'll make the world safe for democracy.
Prove my worth, my equality,
Fight for the land of the free.

Shipped off to France, for the fight eager
Called us a slave unit & gave us hard labor.
      We demanded to fight, but captain said,
      "Sportin' a gun, you'd be struttin', son.
      Why President Wilson, he's a southern one.
      And he fears y'all more than the Hun."
But too many men killed, trenches left vacant.
Finally, one day sent us up to the front.
Germans dropped leaflets: "Your enemy's behind.
Can you sit where whites sit? Can you dine where they dine?"
      But we went over the top & advanced the line.
      We fought the Bush back to the Rhine. *We fought the Bush back to the Rhine.*

Proud to live in the land of the free,
We made the world safe for democracy.
We proved our worth, our equality,
We fought for the land of the free.

France toasted us as heroes.
We danced with French girls & sang with French fellows.

"Stop treating 'em as equals," our General told France.
"Might bring home that notion, can't take that chance.
 Don't salute him or shake his hand,
 Don't even converse with the black man."
  America hadn't changed, but changed had we.
  We'd tasted sweet nectar of equality.
  "We return from fighting. We return fighting,"
  Du Bois said, & some wrongs need righting.
Were homeward-bound 'til the commander's edict:
"We don't allow your kind on our battleship. *Never on our battleship.*"

We're proud to live in the land of the free,
We'll make the U.S. safe for democracy.
We proved our worth, our equality,
We'll fight to make America free.

Went back to Georgia in uniform
To see my mother's smile so warm.
White man approached as I walked there.
"Boy, get off the sidewalk," he angrily declared.
  But I stood my ground, I stood up tall.
  Said, "Fellow American, I just fought for y'all.
  I ain't gonna take your abuse no more.
  To be treated like a slave I didn't fight in that war."
He slapped my face & I shoved back.
Police only arrested the only one black.
Men lynched me in the town square.
Women looked on as I hung there.
Children played on as I swung there. *As I hung there.*

Two months later, on the 4th of July,
Their white soldiers all paraded by.
Woman and children cheered happily.
While waving the flag of this land of the free.
Right where they lynched me! *Here in the land of the free.*

Life On A String

Fathers & Sons

Father's Day 2015

A fine Father's Day
Though I spent it alone.
Jenny at her college reunion,
To Assateague boys gone.
So proud of each one:
Smarter than their dad,
Show empathy for others,
Often also wiser
(Just like their mother),
And for that I'm glad.

On the phone, I told my father
(Alone, too, mom out of town)
How proud I had been
When, a few years past,
He chose tenderness over anger
With my son Dietre.
And he told me he, too,
Was proud of me as a son.

And we reminisced about Benny,
Dad's old friend in Orange City
Who ran the Phillip's 66
And who, on Dad's last visit,
Long after we had moved away,
Had stopped Dad on the street,
Jumped out of his pickup
To give Dad a big bear hug.

And he thanked me for the
     poems I had sent him
One about an aspect of Orange City
That – fondly – I still think of
And one an apology
For my behavior as a teenager
(Now that my kids are doing to me
– Just a fraction –
Of what I did to him.)

My Father's Day dinner
Was a slice of pizza & soda at Wegmans
While working on a poem about forgiveness
In Charleston, South Carolina,
And, while writing,
Feeling strangely blessed.
I had just hosted the Folk Show,
Sammy Cannillo my guest.

Now sitting on the front porch
Writing this & more,
Pausing to sip a grapefruit shandy
& pet our Gryffindor.
The only sounds in the air
Are the birds & NPR.
Though calling me, silently,
Is my Oriskany guitar.

The Idiot

I know that I'm an idiot, I know that I'm uncool.
Know that I embarrass you, like some old fool.
At 16, son, you're as smart as you'll ever be
And the worst thing for you is to be seen with me.
No more playing board games together Friday nights
Or biking to the park on windy days to try our kites.
'Cause now that you're a teenager, I'm a pariah
I'm senile in my dotage, while you're a high fly-ah.

I understand this phase you're in, for that's just what it is.
I did the same to my own dad, as he did it to his.
So I put up with your rolled eyes and snarky attitude
You probably can't help it - at your age I did it, too.
But I know the day will come when you'll change your mind.
I've still got a few words of wisdom to pass on, you'll find.
Once you're in the real world, you'll find I'm not so dumb.
Need help with your taxes? See how smart I become.

Maybe when you've bought a house, or expecting your first child,
You'll begin to reinterpret all these grievances you've filed.
I may not have been the best parent a child could ever claim,
But some perspective on my failings you might even gain.
Just like me you'll start off planning to be
Everything your own dad wasn't, to be better than he.
Expect you haven't noticed, but I'm still trying to improve
Perhaps by the time you're 30, I'll have found my parental groove.

So keep walking ahead of me, so no one will ever think
We're together, or worse, related, lest their opinion of you sink.
I can't walk as fast as I once could, or as fast as you walk now.
You're striding into your future, one I'll see if God allows.
I'll just plod on behind you, watch you do your thing
And prepare for you to leave and then try not to cling.
'Cause I know you'll be back to visit, to see your old man.
And one of those times I'll no longer be the idiot I now am.
Yeah, one of those times I'll no longer be the idiot I now am.

Playing Catch in Ebbets Field

You grew up cheering those Boys of Summer,
In Ebbets Field, you couldn't be happier.
Jackie Robinson your boyhood hero
But your childhood ended and they fled that Borough.
When I was a boy, we'd play catch for hours,
Recapture your dream of those Brooklyn Dodgers.
Together, dad, we were dreaming hard
While tossing that ball out in the backyard.
Stand on our little hill, I pitched with all my might.
Snap, in your glove, and you called it a strike.
Quit only when it started to get dark
Finally come in from our baseball park.

Chorus: Playin' catch in Ebbets Field
We're Brooklyn Dodgers, or so we feel.
At that moment, everything was fine
Gone were your troubles, and so were mine.
No more dragged down by choices regretted,
Opportunities denied, friendships rejected.
You with your cat in your favorite chair,
We're laughin' at Carson, that evening we'd share.

I must have been a big disappointment
I lived out in right field or just sat on the bench.
Despite all that time you invested in me,
My bein' a ballplayer was just not to be.
Except for the time that I caught that high fly ball
Hit by our town's slugger, it was right at the wall.
As a teenager we fought all the time –
I don't recall why, but I knew the fault was not mine!
I was sure I knew far more than you,
The world was simple and I could see what was true.
Now I'm your age, and it's all cloudy again
Lines are grayer than they were back then.

Chorus

Challenged your students to think on their own,
In our little town, it was somewhat unknown.
Insisted on reading my college papers
More often than not declaring them failures.
"I would have given you a C, too,"
You'd say, but I kept the one you gave an A to.
Posed deep questions, like an iconoclast:
"What's the essence of a chair?"
You were known to ask.
The whole wide world sits on the back of a turtle,
Which sits on another, a tower eternal.
There's more turtles below, to be found,
'Cause it's just turtles all the way down.

Chorus

I've spent my life trying to avoid your mistakes,
Evade your flaws, your regrets escape.
You couldn't lose weight, so I've tried to keep fit
You struggled to quit smoking, so I never lit.
But as I get older, I can't help but see more
Of you in me, we're quite similar at the core.
Now you've trouble walking & had some health scares,
Time has taken me unawares.
Decades have passed, but yet also none,
Now I'm the father, but back then the son.
It's a lovely day, boy, go grab your mitt
Let's go in the back & throw the ball a bit.

Let's play some catch out in Ebbets Field
We'll be Brooklyn Dodgers, a moment we'll steal.
I promise you, son, everything will be fine
Gone will be your troubles, and so will be mine.

Life On A String

Things We Forget

My old phone number, where I left my keys
Lyrics to that old song, bands from the '80s.
Computer commands on the Commodore 64
That girl I liked back in '84.
Password to the website I rarely use
Why the hell I bought those blue-suede shoes.
A cutting remark for that jerk at work
That cool line uttered by Captain Kirk.

Things we forget, memories brittle
Losing our past, little by little.
The images are flighty, gone in a blink
Back to the depths of memory they sink.
Some we're relieved to let go,
Others we clutch onto from long ago.

House I lived in when I was five
Eagerly awaiting Christmas to arrive.
Playing whiffle ball in the backyard.
Beating up the bully who pushed me too hard.
Mountains of snow we loved to climb
How it felt to kiss you that first time.
Our son just born, what an amazing sight
Singing him to sleep every night.

Things we forget, memories brittle
Losing our past, little by little.
The images are flighty, gone in a blink
Back to the depths of memory they sink.
Kids grow up & we struggle to remember
All that happened when they were younger.

Watching polar bears & seals at the Zoo
Our endless games of Peek-a-boo.
Pi to ten places at two you memorized
Always wanted 3 more times down the slide.
Sneaking grass to the sheep at Mount Vernon
Red Elmo doll your constant companion.
Little word games we'd play at bedtime
Laughing while saying a silly rhyme.

Things we forget, memories brittle
Losing our past, little by little.
The images are flighty, gone in a blink
Back to the depths of memory they sink.
Some we wish would never go,
Others still haunt us from long ago.

Joining in picking on that kid on the playground
Glad I wasn't the victim this time around.
To impress that girl, I acted like a fool
And all those many times I lost my cool.
Memories dredged up we wish to bury
We can be our own harshest jury.
Hurtful words spoken in anger
Forgiveness given, but hurt feelings linger.

Things we forget, memories brittle
Losing our past, little by little.
The images are flighty, gone in a blink
Back to the depths of memory they sink.
The mind sure is a tricky thing
Both joy and sadness it can bring.
Warm the heart or the ego sting,
Too often good old memories take wing.

Life On A String

An Autumn Hike

Muted sunlight struggles through gaps in the clouds,
Stark tree trunks painted against the gray sky.
Their leaves all fallen, crunching 'neath our feet,
A reminder of how quickly time can fly by.
It's a cold day in November & I'm hiking with my son.

A babe in my arms, 'til I looked up and you were
Running 'round the house in your light-up shoes.
Yelling "Super Dietre!" then jumping down the stairs
Fervently painting, driven by a muse.
With duct tape & Legos, you could build anything.
Feels like just yesterday that it was spring.

A fine young man here walking by my side.
You're quiet, miss nothing, your thoughts run deep.
Rejoice how you do things in your own unique way,
Yet look at you with both sadness and pride.
'Cause I see others rein in your creative soul,
How the world buffets you 'round, exerts its control.

Once we'd collect acorns, white, red, pin, & burr oak,
& you'd sniff the walnut fruit & hickory nuts.
Winter now approaches, mostly brown to see, 'cept
Flashes of red & yellow amid evergreen trees.
It's a cold day in November & I'm hiking with my son.

A time for reflection, on thoughts intertwined,
Of you first climbing our front yard tree.
Yet the greater the joys, the deeper the regrets.
You called out, "Daddy, Come play with me."
Busy grading papers, I said once I was done.
If only could undo some choices, my son.

When did we stop reading together at night?
So many more books I wanted to share.
But you've outgrown that now like so much else.
Let's read a book this evening, I'd suggest, but don't dare.
Won't be long before college & you've gone away,
But around Shaver's Creek, we're roaming today.

Was cleaning out the garage, sorting a pile of old toys
And I recalled how we used to play out in the backyard.
I thought of you inside in your video game funk
And I asked, "Why am I in here messing with this junk?"
So I yelled, "Grab your coat, let's go on a hike!
Or shoot hoops, ride bikes, whatever you'd like."

So now we're circling Lake Perez, jackets zipped tight,
Crossin' over the dam, see a hawk in flight.
Shadows grown long & we've nothing more to say
(Or what we have left is too complex for this day).
It's a cold day in November & I'm hiking with my son.

Soon you'll be leaving to take on the world.
Will you be happy & safe? I ask with concern.
But this fearing the future just takes away
From the joy of the moment & gives naught in return.
So won't worry about the road ahead that neither of us can see.
'Cause right now, you're here, hiking with me.

We'll stop at Harner Farm when we drive by
For some hot apple cider & a fresh apple pie.
Sit & sip & look out at their Christmas trees
Warm our insides while our noses freeze.
Then back to my work, you back to your game
But this brief time together, we've managed to claim.
It's a cold day in November & I'm hiking with my son.

Life On A String

A Father's Love For His Son

Pastor looked haggard this Sunday morn.
Benediction over, yet kept up his arms.
As if to say, "Please stay in the pews."
A pregnant pause, then gave us this news:

When my son was born 30 years ago,
I felt God saying, "I love you so.
I'm a God of grace, do you not see?
Now love and care for this child for me."

To raise him as God wills, I always have yearned,
But too often His voice's been hard to discern.
Gets lost amidst the static of daily life,
Of sermons, committees, and petty strife.

So when my son came out to me earlier this year,
I felt betrayed and I reacted with fear.
How had I sinned? Where had I erred?
As a father, as a pastor, I so despaired.
How could God do this to my only child?
I prayed to God to fix him, while I lived in denial.
I begged God to fix him, my only child.

Then I dreamed one night I was at heaven's gates
And there Saint Peter himself did wait.
He demanded of me to give account
Of all my deeds, all my thoughts recount.
He never once asked whom I failed to chastise,
But inquired about each time I ignored cries
Failed to heal the hurting, to show God's love.
Instead I condemned, too eager to judge.
Instead I condemned, too eager to judge.

I realized then how it must have cut deep.
Things I'd said, things I'd preached.
And I finally saw him clearly as his God-given self,
Not the mold I'd created, a mirror of myself.
Now he's asked me for more, and this is my test:
Consecrate his marriage, his union bless.
"You'll be defrocked," the Bishop's made clear.
"Such flouting of Church Rule is most severe."

But God gave me a son, and that child I will love,
I hope and pray with blessings from above.
I sure could be wrong, and part of me says I am,
But it's the selfish, frightened part of this man.
That same Christ in whom my trust I place
Will forgive me for erring on the side of grace.
Will forgive me for erring on the side of grace.

'Cause one day in Heaven, I could never defend
Rejecting my son, to the devil him send.
I'd rather justify my lifting him up
To my God, I'll drink from that cup.
He may be a sinner, but I am one, too
& I'm his father, and so this I must do.
And if anyone knows placing love over law
It's the Jesus from whom my strength I draw.
That Jesus who died to place love over law.

Then he stood there, waiting, while we all sat stunned.
I didn't know what to say, just turned to my son.
A dear little angel, in that pew taking a nap.
Kissed his cheek, then stood up and clapped.
I can't argue theology, never been to seminary,
But God Himself has a son born to Mary.
So I know even God feels love for a Son.
Yes, our God sure knows a father's love for his Son.
Yes, our God knows a father's love for his Son.

Life On A String

Random Walks

Late at night in San Francisco,
In my Honda with my best friend
Strike out in a random direction
Drive and drive for hours on end.
Open to finding new places
Going down roads we've never ridden'
Serendipity may find us
Listen to hear if she's biddin'.
Not all who wander are lost
Choose a path that meanders
Stop and talk with a stranger
Share your story, but reflect on hers.

I speak a kind word to a nervous
Child, she beams validated.
Her smile is the most beautiful
Sight I've seen so far today.
A knowing wink or pat on the shoulder
From my father now I'm grown
Means far more than any honor
Especially with two sons of my own.
No one is extraneous
In one large family we all are bound
Show love to each other
Build them up not tear them down.

My son just turned fifteen
Where those years went I can't conceive.
Rejoice as he 'comes independent
Yet reminded someday he'll leave.
Baby crawling after the cats
Scooter boy at one and a half
Tickle-tackle on the family room rug
Searching for Blues Clues with my bug.
Children are the greatest paradox
Each new age is filled with joy
Yet also tinged with regret:
This young man was once my little boy.

Looking back o'er the path I've taken
Change has been my firm companion.
Choose to fight or blend with it
But recognize that nothing's certain.
As I've flowed though my life
Things that once seemed so important
Are revealed to be mere ephemera
In all this change I find what's constant:
Love God & love your neighbor
As yourself, forgive not condemn,
Everyone is a child of God
What you do to them you do to Him.
What you do to them you do to Him.

Farewell

Life On A String

Uncle Jim

Sitting on plastic chairs
On the back-yard slab,
Spinnin' tales of Wells Fargo,
Gold and Indian raids.
"This year I'll find that gold
& take you away from here,
Treasure hunters we will be,
Bold fearless & brave."

Born in Iowa, shot in Korea
A bullet in his head, he was left for dead.
They ran him through laying on the ground
He did not flinch, made no sound.
His buddies came for him that night,
Helicoptered out by moonlight.
I'm so glad that they saved him,
For he became my Uncle Jim.
… someday we'd be …

Sitting on plastic chairs,
Just me & Uncle Jim.
Spinnin' tales of Wells Fargo,
Gold and Indian raids.
"This year I'll find that gold
& take you away from here,
Treasure hunters we will be,
Bold fearless & brave."

Scarred by war, would go explore,
An endless font of western lore.
On the trail of long-lost gold,
He worked his claim for hours untold.
Every summer he'd pass through,
Full of old legends he swore were true.
Though the stories never changed,
I never doubted what he claimed.
… 'cause we were …

Sitting on plastic chairs,
Soaking up the July heat,
Spinnin' tales of Wells Fargo,
Gold and Indian raids.
"This year I'll find that gold
& take you away from here,
Treasure hunters we will be,
Bold fearless & brave."

At Crater Lake he found his treasure,
My Aunt Lois, his love forever.
In later years, a hospital orderly,
Eased his patients by telling his stories.
Caught me shooting BB's at birds,
"Killing's not a sport," were his words.
Showed me how to treat a snake bite,
Taught me poker & we played 'til midnight.
… and we'd be …

Sitting on plastic chairs,
On a July eve,
Spinnin' tales of Wells Fargo,
Gold and Indian raids.
"This year I'll find that gold
& take you away from here,
Treasure hunters we will be,"
He promises as the sunlight fades.

No more a boy, I've grown old
And I no longer believe in that gold.
But I still dream, I confess,
That we're prospecting way out west.
Ghost towns and treasure maps,
Old mines about to collapse.
Uncle Jim, let's embark on that quest,
… But it's too late, he's gone to his rest.
… I wish we were …

Sitting on plastic chairs,
For just one more time.
Spinnin' tales of Wells Fargo,
Gold and Indian raids.
"This year I'll find that gold
& take you away from here,
Treasure hunters we will be,"
He promises as the sunlight fades.

Somewhere his gold sits, waiting until
& Somewhere out there his spirit searches still.

Joe Strummer

Heard you fought the law with the Last Gang in Town.
Rocked the Casbah, never worked for the Clampdown.
Yeah, Some Punk Valhalla I'm sure you went to,
But John Mellor, London's still Calling you.
Those Washington Bullets and Rudy Can't Fail
Your music, my youth, an entangled tale.
Now I'm Lost in the Supermarket, but then hear you play.
Yeah, without you, Joe, I'm so Bored with the U. S. A.

The only band that mattered, at least in my day.
Ivan meets GI Joe as Spanish Bombs play.
"Should I Stay or Should I Go?" Radio Clash transmits.
Think of you and Joe Ely when hear Mick yell "Split!"
"Without people you're nothin'," you wisely said,
As you cleaned your black guitar in the City of the Dead.
Could have had my name on that credits list,
But now I'm just a physicist.

"The future's unwritten," so you said, Joe.
When death kicked on your front door, how did you go?
Take that lift from the Four Horsemen?
Did you Lose that Skin you were imprisoned in?
Made you King of the Ramshackle Day Parade,
As you Clashed into the next world unafraid.
Did you heed the Call-Up, or did you stay free?
Was it Death or Glory, did you stand by me?

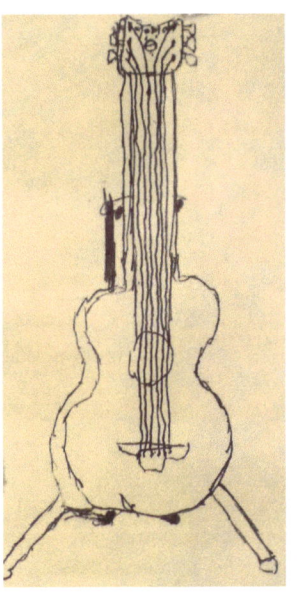

Your Coma Girl's beating Global a Go-Go,
A Phoenix reborn, you Mescalero.
Like Johnny Appleseed, spread Silver & Gold,
Your soul, no one can say, you ever sold.
You sang 'bout Redemption with that Man in Black
Then you passed on and never looked back.
But in our hearts, Joe, you'll never be gone.
As long as we've breath, we'll sing your songs.
Yeah as long as we've breath (and guitars, too),
We'll be singing (and playing) your songs.

Raspberry Jam

Sparkling eyes.
Crooked wry smile.
Horn-rimmed glasses.
Infectious cackle.

Quirky love songs
Cracking me up.
Stink bugs & bananas
Wood sticks & cow bones.

So bow your fiddle
& boogie with me.
Come bugle boy
Of Company B.

Now streaked silver hair's
Collapsed in laughter.
Blow me a raspberry.
I'll see you next year.

Be A Man (Mr. Rogers)

Troubles so rife, sought escape from this life.
Cut by her laugh, how she twisted the knife.
Been stabbed by his jab, "Boy, Learn to be a man."
Punched a deep nerve, I didn't understand.
Now seething & seeking wisdom from a can.
Flipping TV channels to learn to be a man.

Six-pack now gone & there before my eyes
Mr. Roger's Neighborhood, a surreal surprise.
Cry "Why's he still on?" & toss a can at the wall.
His sneakers, his sweater, why I mock 'em all.
How he hung up his coat, not threw it over a chair.
I mock his soft voice, no manhood there.

Why you can escape to your land of make believe,
But here in the real world, there is no reprieve.
My days dissipated, nights drunk & cruel,
You see good in others, but I ain't no fool.

Yet something keeps me watching, like I am mesmerized
Memories long buried flow to my surprise.
Slapped down by a father who only spoke with his belt,
So I hardened inside 'til I no longer felt.
I turned fifteen & away he just ran
Left me adrift – on how to be a man.

Mr. Rogers, Mr. Rogers, oh how did you know?
Can't believe I'm watching your show.
But my life's just a vortex of violence and hate,
Spiraling into the shadows at an increasing rate,
So I need your calm voice before it's too late.

In a sudden stark light, see the choices I'd made
Girls I discarded once my passion did fade.
That son I've never met and probably never will.
Cursed by my father, so that curse I've fulfilled.
Say you want to be my neighbor?
That I doubt you would choose.
If you knew all I'd done, you'd surely refuse.

Mr. Rogers, Mr. Rogers, oh why did you go?
Didn't you know I still need you so?
'Cause my life's been a vortex of violence & hate,
Behind me is trailing a pain-fueled wake,
So I need your calm voice before it's too late.

In this day & age, what does it mean to be a man?
Such conflicting notions, so hard to understand.
But as I watch you now, I begin to grasp
That there's another path to be a man.

'Cause I see how you are a man so strong
To make all you meet feel they belong.
How you lift up those who pass your way.
"Give of yourself & be kind," you say.
Dare I veer down this road, do you think that I can?
Am I strong enough to be this kind of man?

Mr. Rogers, Mr. Rogers, oh why did you go?
Didn't you know we still need you so?
Amid the cacophony of violence & hate,
In a world this adrift we just can't wait,
We need men like you before it's too late.
In a world so adrift through violence & hate,
We need men like you before it's too late.

Life On A String

Sarah Jane

We lusted after Lela, that sexy Severteem.
She could sure fight, how she wielded that knife.
Romana was perky, a brilliant Time Lord.
But you, Sarah Jane, were the one we adored.
On top of our list, Sarah Jane Smith.

Chorus:
Sarah Jane, oh Sarah Jane,
How we love you Sarah Jane!
Sarah Jane, oh Sarah Jane,
How we miss you Sarah Jane!

Stopped Sutek on the Pyramids of Mars,
Invasions of Androids & Dinosaurs,
Sontarans in the future & times medieval,
Monster of Peladon & Planet of Evil.
Faced the Revenge of the Cybermen.

Stood up to the Doctor when you met,
Then snuck into his TARDIS to be the finest yet.
At first didn't trust him, but were true to the end.
More than traveling companion, the Doctor's sure friend.
Since Totter's Lane, none like Sarah Jane.

An intrepid investigative journalist,
Brave, not scheming like Adric.
Spunky, not whiny like Tegan,
But Gallifrey called & he left you then.
Without Sarah Jane, The Doctor was never the same.

Chorus

Thought he'd forgotten you & moved on then,
But at School Reunion, so happy to see you again.
Learned you'd been active, oh we should have known,
You were defending the Earth from Bannerman Road.
You & Mr. Smith & your sonic lipstick.

But why, Sarah Jane, did you leave us so quick?
Lis Sladen & Ms. Smith, you are both deeply missed.
Lis, though you're gone, Sarah Jane lives on
Treasured by millions, especially this one.
The greatest it's plain, you were, Sarah Jane.

Chorus

As you once said about Eldrid,
Sarah Jane must live!

River Song
*For River Song, who passed away
a mere 2 years old on May 3, 2015*

Jacob's Patronus just passed away
His feline doppelganger left us today.
That River ran fast, that River ran strong,
A real shame that he couldn't run long.

From a litter born to a neighborhood stray,
Picked him for his mottled steel gray.
The hissing of Crookshanks he fearlessly faced.
A paper bag or basket his favorite place.
Peaches cries out, looking for his friend.
No way to explain to him how it did end.

Now our boys in tears we can't console &
We're reminded how little we can control.
Jenny reads Owl & the Pussycat beneath the full moon
While I hug Dietre who bemoans, "He left us too soon!"

River Song, I'd ask you what's on that other side.
But "Spoilers!" you'd say (in cat tongue)
"It'd ruin the ride."

Life On A String

The Secret

"Be like Steve"
– you, not me –
I ponder,
 as I exit the observatory
 & wander
 along the nature trail,
 the evening air refreshing
 after our sips of brandy.

 My parting question:
"What's the secret?"
"Be yourself," your reply.
 But that secret still elusive
 twenty-four years
 since I last
 left you here.

Photo Credits:

All photographs are taken by the author (and copyright by the author) except where noted. All photographs by others are used with permission.

Cover: Drawing by Dietre Van Hook
- i. Author performing incidental music at the Central Pennsylvania Festival of the Arts (State College, Pennsylvania) by invitation of Jim Colbert. Photo by Jim Colbert.
- iii. James Read (Uncle Jim). Painting by Lois Read.
- v. Point Reyes National Seashore (California).
- vi. Loch Ness, Scotland.
- 1. *La Grande Vitesse* by Alexander Calder in Grand Rapids, Michigan.
- 2. *East Wing Mobile* by Alexander Calder (National Gallery of Art, Washington, DC).
- 4. Bradley Beach, New Jersey, at sunrise.
- 5. Ocean Grove, New Jersey, at sunrise.
- 6. Jim Colbert performing at Tait Farm, Centre Hall, Pennsylvania.
- 7. Statue of Lucy Lederer (by her son Eugene Lederer) in Lederer Park, State College, Pennsylvania.
- 7. Angel Soto practicing Tai Chi sword in Lederer Park, State College, Pennsylvania.
- 8. Dietre Van Hook flying a stunt kite at Holland State Park, Michigan.
- 10. Author and Joe Belle at Webster's Bookstore & Café, State College, Pennsylvania. Photo by Jennifer Van Hook.
- 11. Author's cat Peaches on a piano bench.
- 12. Cross on church in Nuremberg, Germany.
- 14. Cardinal at Mount Vernon (Virginia). Photo by Jacob Van Hook.
- 15. Fresnel lens at the Pigeon Point Lighthouse at Point Reyes National Seashore (California).
- 16. The Very Large Array (VLA) radio interferometer outside Socorro, New Mexico.
- 18. Alley in Edinburgh, Scotland.
- 19. Cologne Cathedral, Germany.
- 20. Author's 2013 American Lives album cover, designed and drawn by Dietre Van Hook.
- 22. Jon Vickers-Jones performing at Webster's Bookstore & Café (State College, Pennsylvania).
- 23. Stone circle in Avebury, England.
- 24. Dietre, Jenny, and Jacob Van Hook with Gryffindor the dog.
- 25. Rothenburg ob der Tauber, Germany.
- 27. Jenny Van Hook and our first car, a Honda Civic (Point Lobos, California).
- 29. Jacob Van Hook kayaking (Bellefonte, Pennsylvania).
- 31. Tree on path to the Pigeon Point Lighthouse at Point Reyes National Seashore (California).
- 32. Lamp in snowstorm (State College, Pennsylvania).
- 34. Cross in graveyard outside Dornoch Cathedral (Scotland).
- 35. Graveyard at Gettysburg National Cemetery (Pennsylvania).
- 36. Flying buttress by roof of York Minster (York, England).
- 38. Berlin (Germany) Train Station.

39. Mary Van Hook at the Harry P. Leu Gardens (Orlando, Florida).
40. Jennifer Van Hook in rock garden (State College, Pennsylvania).
42. Henry Lincoln Johnson with his Croix de Guerre in 1918. Image is in the public domain in the United States (published before 1923).
47. Neuschwanstein Castle (Bavaria, Germany) built by "Mad King" Ludwig II.
49. Stream from waterfall leading into Pacific Ocean at Point Reyes National Seashore (California)
51. Lincoln Memorial in Washington, DC.
52. Author with his father and two sons in the Poconos (Pennsylvania).
55. Dietre and Jacob Van Hook hiking at Point Reyes National Seashore (California).
56. Jay Van Hook giving a lecture at the University of Zimbabwe.
56. Jay Van Hook with our cat Magie in Orange City, Iowa. Photo by Mary Van Hook.
57. Jay Van Hook amused by a paper in Orange City, Iowa. Photo by Mary Van Hook.
59. Jacob Van Hook at Mount Vernon (Virginia).
60. Dietre Van Hook jumping down stairs (Bowling Green, Ohio).
61. Dietre Van Hook hiking at Yosemite National Park (California), with orangutan at Toledo Zoo (Ohio).
62. Labyrinth in Brookside Gardens (Wheaton, Maryland). Photo by Jacob Van Hook.
63. Cross over Freiburg, Germany.
65. James Read (Uncle Jim). Photo taken by Barbara Read.
67. James Read (Uncle Jim) in 1952. Photographer unknown.
68. Sketch of guitar by Dietre Van Hook when he started learning guitar.
69. Dietre Van Hook first learning guitar.
70. Statue in Rothenburg ob der Tauber, Germany.
72. Dalek drawing by Dietre Van Hook from when he was nine or ten years old.
73. Author and sons wearing Doctor Who bathrobes.
74. Jacob Van Hook and River Song. Photo by Jacob Van Hook.
75. River Song in basket. Photo by Jennifer Van Hook.
76. Strawbridge Observatory at Haverford College (Pennsylvania).
79. Yosemite National Park (California).

Life On A String

www.ingramcontent.com/pod-product-compliance
Lightning Source LLC
Chambersburg PA
CBHW041537220426
43663CB00002B/63